To Seek His Fortune

by Mona McElderry

illustrated by Kate Furler

SISU Press
New York Mills MN

1994
SISU Press
101 East Gilman Street
New York Mills MN 56567

Printed in the United States of America.

Library of Congress Catalog Card Number:
96-66997

ISBN 0-9641573-0-6

1. Adolescent independence – psychology 2. Parental bonds – psychology 3. Empty nest – psychology 4. Play therapy – psychology 5. Pet therapy – psychology

A word from Tom:

My mother has written that most rare book in the age of the super-novel – one that is at once brief, simple, and complex. She has used modern language in the form of the traditional fable to deliver her message straight to the heart.

In preparing *To Seek His Fortune* for press, we have found ourselves disagreeing on whether to include hot issues like drug abuse, promiscuity, and AIDS: the "dogs" that hound every young person searching for identity. But in the end, my mother opted for a timeless theme. My adventures in college will remain peripheral to this story of immediate loss and enduring love.

We hope that *To Seek His Fortune* will bring joy and comfort to other families who find their paths diverging. Through separation and reunion, our family has discovered that the generation gap is not so wide after all, and that there is very little we can't get through with a little understanding and a lot of tongue bathing.

Tom McElderry

To families everywhere:

I wrote *To Seek His Fortune* in 1990
when my son, Tom, was packing for college
and I was crying my eyes out.

He has since survived dying his hair blue
and being disciplined for spending the night
in the girls' dorm.

You don't want to see
your son or daughter leave
but you know they must.

It's time for your youngster to seek his fortune.
Let go, my friend.

Love,
Mona

To Seek His Fortune

**Not long ago,
in a place not far away**

there was a young man named Tom

who decided that it was time
to go off
to seek his fortune.

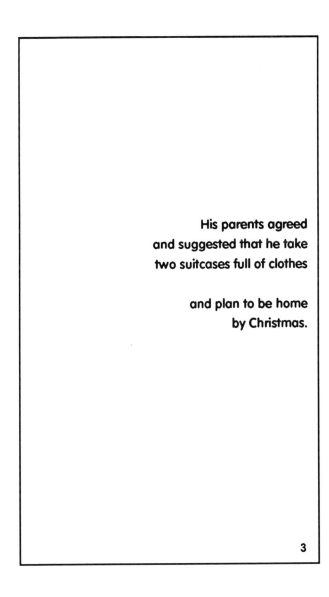

His parents agreed
and suggested that he take
two suitcases full of clothes

and plan to be home
by Christmas.

But his cats, Bagel and Ditty, were concerned.

That evening as Tom lay
on his waterbed,
Bagel considered how to instruct him.

She closed her eyes as she thought of
all the dogs out in the world.

"Anyone who licks your face
is trying too hard
to be friendly,"
she counseled.
"You have to ask yourself
why.

Either you're pretty

or
they're trying to sell you something.

And I have to break it to you, Tom,
you're almost completely
hairless."

"Be careful what you eat," Ditty continued.
"Just because it can be swallowed
doesn't mean it belongs in your belly!

Right, Bagel?"

Bagel turned her face away,
recalling
with embarrassment
some of her past gastronomic misadventures.

They really were quite fond of Tom,
having followed him
across the country to four different houses,
and they hated to see him go.

"Don't drink cold water," Ditty ordered.
Both Bagel and Tom waited for her explanation.

They knew she only drank
warm water from Tom's bath
every morning
but had never understood why.

"If you drink someone's bath water,"
Ditty began,
"and sit on the edge of the tub
and watch them take their bath,
that will give you time
to start the day
by feeling loved.

That's the important thing."

She flipped her tail for emphasis.

Tom knew that was how Ditty lived her life.

She was a most loving animal.

Although he had never wanted
to taste bath water,
he decided to take seriously
her suggestion

that he start each morning
by feeling loved.

He considered for a bit
how he would manage that
so far from
his loving cats.

They had never been good
at writing letters.

Ditty was watching his face.
She sensed his dilemma.
I will always love you," she said firmly.

She lay down then
on his chest
and half-closed her eyes.
Bagel arranged herself neatly
at the foot of the waterbed.

Tom put one hand
on Ditty's silky fur
and fell quickly asleep.

While he slept,
Ditty and Bagel
discussed the situation at length.

"He's really too young to go," Bagel insisted.

"He's young," Ditty agreed.
"But,
he can run fast,
hide well,
catch anything he needs,
and keep himself clean."

"You didn't remind Tom
to get to bed promptly,"
Bagel chided.

"I knew he wouldn't anyway,"
Ditty replied.

"Staying up late is a necessary part
of this adventure.

Sometimes the most strange and wondrous
things are seen by sleep-heavy eyes."

"Is it habit forming?" Bagel asked.

"Usually," Ditty replied mildly.
"But it's okay.
When Tom comes home,
he will sleep for three days and nights
and then

he will be our Tom again."

"Are you sure this is necessary?" Bagel asked.

"Well, yes!" Ditty said.
"It's only after keeping many an all-night vigil
that he is apt to meet
a unicorn."

"A unicorn!" Bagel exclaimed.
"There aren't any unicorns anymore."

"Not in this neighborhood," Ditty agreed.
And then she added,
"Oh, yes!
And he may even bring one home sometime."

Bagel was speechless.
She blinked a number of times
and had to get a drink of water for herself.

When she returned
Ditty saw that she had been crying.
"He doesn't really love us,"
she told Ditty.

"He would never want to leave us
if he did."

"That's not true," Ditty said.

"He has loved me
since I was a kitten,

and you
he loved
from the very beginning
when you were born on his brothers' bed.

He is not leaving us.

He's going off
to seek his fortune.

He will be back.

But more important than that,
we will go with him
in his heart

and he will be here with us
in our hearts.

Whenever I hear you purr,
I will know you are thinking of Tom.

When he thinks of us,
we will know it.

We will continue to listen
for the sounds he makes when he opens the
door
and drops his coat on the floor."

We will remember.

31

I don't want to remember," Bagel pouted.
"I want him to stay."

This is an investment
we're making,"
Ditty explained.

"Tom is off
to seek his fortune.

When he returns there will be
more of Tom
to love.

He will have new stories to tell,
songs to sing,
friends for us to meet.

His room
will once more be full of exciting sounds
and smells
and sights."

Bagel started to feel
sad again
and she hated to feel sad.

"Let's go beat up Harley," she suggested.

Harley was the alley cat
that lived behind the neighbor's house.

He was not really a stray
because someone gave him food and water
every day

but they did not let him sleep inside
on the beds
or carry him about
or call him "precious"
or introduce him to their friends.

He was just a big yellow cat
who sometimes came up on their porch
to see if Ditty and Bagel wanted to play.

"No, Bagel," said Ditty softly.
"You don't need to be mean to Harley.
It's not his fault.

Just sit here quietly with me.
It's OK to feel sad about Tom."

Bagel closed her eyes.
Her face looked soft and peaceful.
Ditty thought she had gone to sleep
but Bagel was thinking.
Abruptly,
she spoke again.

"What's a fortune?
Tom's going off
to seek his fortune.

What will he find?"

"We know what sort of lad Tom is.
He will find more
of what he already has,"
said Ditty.

"What is that?" Bagel asked.

"Courage," Ditty answered.
"Courage
and truth
and love."

"He has those already," Bagel said.

"Yes, but he needs to exercise them
so they'll grow.

He has loved us for a long time
and we have seen his courage
from the first.

But now
he needs to give it
to the rest of the world."

"Why?" Bagel asked.

"Because it's time," Ditty said.

"Courage is not an easy thing to store.
If you pretend that you don't have it,
if you put it away for awhile,
then when you want it again,
it might be gone.

The same is true for love –
and song
and truth."

Bagel folded her paws under her
so she looked like a cat without legs.

"Will he really come back to us?" she asked.

"Tom knows where we are
and he will always come back,
over and over again,
with more stories
and songs
and truth
and love.

He will come back because
we are a part of him -
the part that makes him strong
and able to seek his fortune.

Go to sleep now, Bagel,
and I will sing you a little song."

Bagel closed her eyes
as Ditty began to purr softly.

"Hush-a-bye. Don't you cry.
Go to sleep, little Bagel.
Sleep and dream,
and when you wake,
know that you are loved,
yes loved,
so loved!"

To Seek His Fortune

is a gift.
All profits from the sale of *To Seek His Fortune*
are donated to the scholarship fund of
Simon's Rock of Bard College.

ORDER FORM

Telephone orders: **1-800-778-7892**
Call Toll Free   *Have credit card ready*

FAX orders: (218) 385-2560

Postal orders: **SISU Press**
P.O. Box 27
New York Mills MN 56567
(218) 385-2723

Please send to :

NAME: ....

Address: ....

....

NAME: ....

Address: ....

....

Price of each book: $10^{00}

We accept VISA + MASTERCARD

Please add 6.5% Tax for books shipped to a Minnesota address.

Shipping: Book Rate: $1^{15} for one book
$1^{50} for two or more books

First Class: $2^{50} for one book
$3^{00} for two or more books